TRY NOT TO LAUGH CHALLENGE

YEAR OLD
EDITION

JOKE BOOK

Silly Fun Kid
publishing

Thank you for choosing Silly Fun Kid

Silly Fun Kid is a nature comedian, represents the work of comedian friends, they try to send some happiness to the little stars and make them laugh and enjoy reading jokes.

Have a question? please visit
sites.google.com/view/sillyfunkid/books
or
use **QR Code**

to learn more and send us message.

We hope you have a great funny time with this book if you like our books please support us with a review this encourages us to do more things .

Try Not To Laugh Challenge

 # BONUS PLAY!

Join our Joke Club and get the Bonus play PDF!

Simply type THIS URL :

https://sites.google.com/view/sillyfunkid/

free?authuser=0

Or
use QR code

and you will get 20 best Funny jokes!
by Silly Fun Kid

Welcome to the try not Laugh challenge

How to play the game?

The try not to laugh challenge is made up of 10 rounds, every round has 2 jesters, each player has a jester, and should make the second player laugh score to the points.

after completing the 10 rounds add all points and find the winner! "Master"

Round 11 : "THE ROUND GIFT"

the round 11 is the rounds gift which is the champion should get a gift!

Who can play this game?

the try not to laugh challenge is a super fun fast easy game for the family or friends to play together and get tons of laughs!

JOKESTER 1

JOKESTER 1

Rules of
The try laugh challenge

- bring the player's friends or family members, get your pencil, prepare your comedy power.

- determine who's the "jokester1" and "jokester2"

- jokester 1 will hold the book and read the jokes.

- pass the book to jokester 2 read jokes.

- once the round completed score points.

- the same thing until round 11, then add all points to find the champion!

- all these guides you will find on the bottom the pages after.

- give to the champion any gifts!

Ready!
time to play
don't laugh

ROUND

1

JOKESTER 1

what favorite thing does the cow
like to do in the morning?   /1
read moos-paper

what kind of food do dragons like
to eat?   /1
burnt food!

Why did the zombie put his money
in the freezer?   /1
he wanted cold hard cash!

what did the bananas servant say
to the director lemon?
hello sour!   /1

 JOKES TOTAL   /4

JOKESTER 1

What is the thing you find every time have for dinner?
dinner!

/1

What type of haircut do sheep get?
baa-baa cuts!

/1

What is the gift that the shark bought for his wife?
A gold-fish!

/1

where did bees go in the summer?
to the buzzzsea!

/1

 JOKES TOTAL   /4

pass the book to jokester 2! ➡️

JOKESTER 2

why dinosaurs are big?
because they ate pizza island with soda   /1

What do unicorns need in the sea?
Swimwear!   /1

Why are frogs smarts?
Because they eat whatever bugs them!   /1

where did eggs go in the morning?
To take a shower in the pan   /1

 **JOKES TOTAL**   /4

JOKESTER 2

why the zombie did not go to the party?

_____ /1

he felt rotten!

why did the dentist leave his job?
because the world became without teeth!

_____ /1

What do you call a hen that tells the time?

A watch-hen!

_____ /1

What sound does a cow make when they fart?

_____ /1

Cow-boom!

JOKES TOTAL _____ /4

time to add up your points!

SCORE BOARD

In each jokester's add total jokes
points for this round!

JOKESTER 1

/8
_____
TOTAL

JOKESTER 2

/8
_____
TOTAL

_____
ROUND 1 WINNER

ROUND

2

JOKESTER 1

Why did the egg hatch?
he was awakened by his mother's fart!   /1

**What do you call a bird with no
wings and no legs?**
A look!   /1

**What time is it when the alarm
didn't ring?**
Time to get a new alarm!   /1

**How do you know there is a bear
in the fridge?**
The door won't shut!   /1

 **JOKES TOTAL**   /4

JOKESTER 1

Which favorite sport do giraffes like to play?
basketball

/1

What is the hardest part of jumping?
The ground!

/1

There were 5 cats in a plane and one jumped out, how many were left?
None, they were all copycats!

/1

Why do chimpanzees have big nostrils?
Because they have big fingers!

/1

 JOKES TOTAL   /4

pass the book to jokester 2! ➡

JOKESTER 2

What's the best thing to put into ice cream? /1
Your tongue!

Why are spiders smart?
Because they live in schools! /1

Can a kangaroo jump higher than a snake?
Yes, of course, a snake can't jump! /1

Why did the gorilla wear sunglasses to class?
Because her monkeys students were so bright! /1

 **JOKES TOTAL** /4

JOKESTER 2

What favorite party do pigs like to go to?
to the clay party!

/1

What did the ladder say when the monkey reached the top?
Stop!

/1

What is the name of the path shortened by ghosts?
Dead ends!

/1

What is the longest month?
February, because it has 8 letters!

/1

 JOKES TOTAL _____ /4

time to add up your points!

SCORE BOARD

In each jokester's add total jokes
points for this round!

JOKESTER 1

/8
_____
TOTAL

JOKESTER 2

/8
_____
TOTAL

_____
ROUND 1 WINNER

ROUND

3

JOKESTER 1

what do cows like to do at the weekend?

/1

watching moovies!

how did the horse win the race?

farts it before the start of the race

/1

What do you get when you cross a crocodile?

A crocroo.. RUN!

/1

Why are robots do not worry?

They have nerves of steel!

/1

 JOKES TOTAL /4

JOKESTER 1

What is a witch's favorite school subject? /1
broom spelling!

What is the favorite place do flies have a fun time? /1
garbage truck!

What can you catch when it's snowing? /1
A cold!

what do eggs do when angry? /1
they hatch!

 JOKES TOTAL /4

pass the book to jokester 2! ➡

JOKESTER 2

What happened to the gorilla who booked a brain transplant? /1

she changed her mind!

why cold is no faster? /1

because you can catch a cold!

What should you do if it's raining meat? /1

do a barbeque party!

What type of shoes does kangaroo wear? /1

shoes basketball players!

JOKES TOTAL /4

JOKESTER 2

what did the toilet say to another? _____ /1
you're stinky take a shower!

when the sun gets sick what happens to it? _____ /1
temperature rise!

what happens if chicken fart? _____ /1
They lay eggs!

What does a book do when it's cold? _____ /1
Puts on a jacket!

 JOKES TOTAL _____ /4

time to add up your points!

SCORE BOARD

In each jokester's add total jokes points for this round!

JOKESTER 1

/8

_____
TOTAL

JOKESTER 2

/8

_____
TOTAL

_____
ROUND 1 WINNER

ROUND

4

JOKESTER 1

What do you call a dragon with no eyes?
Do-you-think-he-saw-us?

/1

What do you call a camel with one hump?
Pregnant!

/1

why does a panda bear lazily?
because it's snowing every day

/1

What's the difference between roast beef and spaghetti?
Anyone can roast beef!

/1

**JOKES TOTAL**

/4

JOKESTER 1

Why don't sharks eat clowns?
Because they taste funny!

/1

What did the snowman say to another?
it's cold!

/1

What did seaweed do every weekend?
clean the sea!

/1

What do you get when you take a cow to the city games?
A milkshake!

/1

 **JOKES TOTAL** /4

pass the book to jokester 2! ➡

JOKESTER 2

Why do we put candles on the top of a birthday cake?

/1

because a wish requires winds to come true!

why don't turtle hurry?

/1

she doesn't care!

What do you call a funny hen?

A comedi-hen!

/1

What kind of dance does flamingo like it?

flamenco dance!

/1

 **JOKES TOTAL**

/4

JOKESTER 2

What's worse than having diarrhea in class?
Having to spell it!

/1

what did the designer hamburger say to the queen pizza?
you're soo cheezy!

/1

where did fishes spend the summer vacation?
Hawaii island

/1

Why sheep are terrible in math?
because she has wool in her head!

/1

 **JOKES TOTAL** /4

time to add up your points!

SCORE BOARD

In each jokester's add total jokes points for this round!

JOKESTER 1

/8
_____
TOTAL

JOKESTER 2

/8
_____
TOTAL

_____
ROUND 1 WINNER

ROUND

5

JOKESTER 1

Why did the elephant fall on the bike?
It was two tired.

/1

What do lawyers wear to court?
lawsuits dress

/1

What do you call a cow that does karate?
A beef chop.

/1

What do you call a lazy dinosaur?
A dino-snore!

/1

JOKES TOTAL /4

JOKESTER 1

What do elves do in school?
learn the elf-abet.

_____ /1

what did the bacon say to the eggs in the morning?
let's have breakfast

_____ /1

What do you get when you cross a lemon and ice?
A sour ice cream.

_____ /1

where did oranges go in the morning?
to prepare the juice

_____ /1

 **JOKES TOTAL** _____ /4

pass the book to jokester 2! ⟶

JOKESTER 2

why did penguins talk too much?
because they eat ice fish!

/1

why did zombies faint in school?
because the teacher fired a rotten fart!

/1

What did the ant say when it was riding on the elephant's back?
Wheeee!

/1

Why did the invisible ghost turn down the job offer?
He couldn't see himself doing it.

/1

JOKES TOTAL

/4

JOKESTER 2

Why sank the pirate ship?   /1
they were playing cards

What did the monkey say when he
jumped out of the closet?   /1
Supplies!

What did the hat say to the scarf?
I'll go ahead.   /1

Did you hear that I'm reading a
book about fire?   /1
It's impossible to put down.

 **JOKES TOTAL**   /4

time to add up your points!

SCORE BOARD

In each jokester's add total jokes points for this round!

JOKESTER 1

/8
_____
TOTAL

JOKESTER 2

/8
_____
TOTAL

_____
ROUND 1 WINNER

ROUND

6

JOKESTER 1

Why are flies annoying people?
because inconvenience is his passion!

/1

What did the unicorn say after it tripped?
"Help! I've fallen and I can't giddyup!"

/1

How many oranges grow on trees?
All of them!

/1

What did the princess say when her photos did not show up?
Someday my prints will come!

/1

 **JOKES TOTAL**

/4

JOKESTER 1

What is a favorite place for popcorn?
movies!

___/1___

How do you catch a whole group of fish?
invite them to a lunch party!

___/1___

How did the black cats end their fight?
the rat says "stop!"

___/1___

Why do pigs win always playing hockey?
They always hog the puck.

___/1___

 **JOKES TOTAL** ___/4___

pass the book to jokester 2! ➡

JOKESTER 2

what happens to the dog in the summer?
/1
turns up to the hot dog!

why do ghosts come out at night?
to play hide and seek!
/1

what did the snake say to the rat when bumped into it?
sssssssory!
/1

What kind of dance do horses like?
mustang-o!
/1

 JOKES TOTAL /4

JOKESTER 2

Why did the farmer sell his chickens?   /1

Because they kept saying "Bach, Bach, Bach!"

What did the buffalo say to his son when he farts in front of him?   /1

Bison!!!

What do you call ice cream melted?   /1

cream!

A sandwich walks into a sushi restaurant.   /1

The waiter says, "Sorry, we don't serve sandwiches in here."

 **JOKES TOTAL**   /4

time to add up your points!

SCORE BOARD

In each jokester's add total jokes points for this round!

JOKESTER 1

/8

_____

TOTAL

JOKESTER 2

/8

_____

TOTAL

_____

ROUND 1 WINNER

ROUND

7

JOKESTER 1

Why did hens fight pigs every day?
because the smell of their fart is almost killing them!

/1

What does pepper do when he gets angry?
becomes red!

/1

Why did the sardines become white?
he was lying in flour

/1

Why do oranges have to put on sunscreen before they go to the beach?
Because they might peel!

/1

 JOKES TOTAL

/4

JOKESTER 1

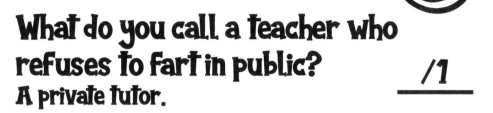

What do you call a teacher who refuses to fart in public?
A private tutor.

/1

What do you call a teacher who refuses to fart in public?
A private tutor.

/1

Why did the zombie go to the hospital?
He was feeling really rotten.

/1

What do you call a monkey with a rubber toe?
monkey Roberto.

/1

 **JOKES TOTAL**   /4

pass the book to jokester 2! ➡

JOKESTER 2

what happens to strawberries when they go to the sea?   /1
became paste!

why did the jungle animal plane fell?   /1
because the plane smelled the elephant fart

What did the dragon say when he sneezed and burned the house?   /1
Oops!

What do you call mummy with no body or nose?   /1
Nobody knows.

JOKES TOTAL   /4

JOKESTER 2

What do you call a cow that can do magic?   /1

A Labracadabracow

How would you feel if a witch stole your mood ring?   /1

You wouldn't know.

How do you turn a soup to gold?   /1

Add 24 potatoes

Why didn't the dinosaur eat the girls?   /1

Because dinosaurs became extinct before humans existed.

 **JOKES TOTAL** /4

time to add up your points!

SCORE BOARD

In each jokester's add total jokes points for this round!

JOKESTER 1

/8

TOTAL

JOKESTER 2

/8

TOTAL

ROUND 1 WINNER

ROUND

8

JOKESTER 1

Why can't dinosaurs dance?
Because they're dead.

/1

What's yellow and something you shouldn't eat?
A school bus.

/1

Why did pirates do piercings?
it's fashion!

/1

Why did the squirrel drink so many cups of coffee?
because he did not fond the nuts!

/1

 **JOKES TOTAL**

/4

JOKESTER 1

What is the method of transportation preferred by bees to travel?   /1

By buzzz!

Why wasn't the geometry teacher at school?   /1

Because the square broke its rib!

What do you call an exploding dinosaur?   /1

A dino -BOOM.

What do you call a bull who is never fun to hang out with?   /1

A cow!

 JOKES TOTAL   /4

pass the book to jokester 2! ➡

JOKESTER 2

What did pigs ask in the restaurant?   /1
cow dung cake

What is the favorite place did the sheep like to go?   /1
The baaaahamas!

What do you call a chimpanzee with a banana in both his ears?   /1
Anything you want, it can't hear you!

How do you stop a parrot from talking in the backseat of a car?   /1
Put it in the front seat.

 **JOKES TOTAL**   /4

JOKESTER 2

How do you catch a rabbit?
send him a smart carrot

_/1

where do ducks go on Friday night?
to the quack quack party!

_/1

what did the winter say to summer?
it's cold!

_/1

Why did the lazy rat want a job in a bakery?
So he could loaf around!

_/1

 **JOKES TOTAL** _/4

time to add up your points!

SCORE BOARD

In each jokester's add total jokes points for this round!

JOKESTER 1

/8
_____
TOTAL

JOKESTER 2

/8
_____
TOTAL

_____
ROUND 1 WINNER

ROUND

9

JOKESTER 1

What do you call a flying fireman?
A helicopter!   /1

What did one tooth say to the other tooth?
I'm sick. I ate a lot of sweets!   /1

What do you call a weight lifting bull?
A bull-dozer.   /1

What do you get from a cow she move a lot?
milkshake!   /1

 **JOKES TOTAL**   /4

JOKESTER 1

Why pizza is delicious?
because she has a cheesy base on social media

/1

Why did the duck cross the road?
To prove he wasn't chicken!

/1

What did the little monkey say when he saw a fart mummy?
mommy!!

/1

How do you know carrots are good for your eyes?
because rabbits do not wear glasses

/1

 **JOKES TOTAL** /4

pass the book to jokester 2! ➡

JOKESTER 2

What is gorilla's favorite dance style?
Hip-Hop!

/1

Why are dragons not lucky?
They burn everything!

/1

Waiter, this food tastes kind of funny?
We put some clowns on it!

/1

Why is the snail late for eating?
Because he doesn't like fast food!

/1

 **JOKES TOTAL** /4

JOKESTER 2

What do you call angry chocolate?
Hot chocolate! /1

If a crocodile makes shoes, what
does a chimpanzee make?
Slippers! /1

How do cows make a milkshake?
They go to the dancing party!

Why are rabbits so lucky? /1
They have a carrot mascot!

/1

 JOKES TOTAL /4

time to add up your points!

SCORE BOARD

In each jokester's add total jokes points for this round!

JOKESTER 1

/8
_____
TOTAL

JOKESTER 2

/8
_____
TOTAL

_____
ROUND 1 WINNER

ROUND

10

JOKESTER 1

Why did the queen go to the dentist?
To get her teeth crowned!

/1

What did baby mummy call her mother?
mommy mummy!

/1

Why don't they serve chocolate in prison?
Because it makes you melt!

/1

What did the English pen say to the Chinese pen?
So, what's your point!

/1

 **JOKES TOTAL**   /4

JOKESTER 1

why you have to go to school every day?
to kill time in school!

___/1___

Which side of the pony has the most hair?
The outside!

___/1___

What kind of meals do math teachers like to eat?
triangle meals!

___/1___

why rats do like to live in houses?
because houses are so cheesy!

___/1___

 JOKES TOTAL ___/4___

pass the book to jokester 2! ➡

JOKESTER 2

Who is the king of the school supplies?   /1
The ruler!

What would you do if a dinosaur sat in front of you at a movie?   /1
Miss most of the film.

What is a mosquito's favorite subject at school?   /1
Mothematics.

What do you do when you see a skate elephant?   /1
Get out of its way!

 JOKES TOTAL   /4

JOKESTER 2

what is chicken a favorite movie?
corn in wonderland!   /1

what happened when skunks were angry?
fart an explosive bomb!   /1

what cat's favorite hobby?
scratch everything!   /1

what do you do if an elephant farts it?   /1
just run go away!

 **JOKES TOTAL**   /4

time to add up your points!

SCORE BOARD

In each jokester's add total jokes points for this round!

JOKESTER 1

/8
_____
TOTAL

JOKESTER 2

/8
_____
TOTAL

_____
ROUND 1 WINNER

ROUND

11

ROUND
GIFT

JOKESTER 1

What did the tooth say to the dentist as she was leaving?
don't leave my place blank!

/1

where did the fishes go Saturday night?
to watch scary sharks movie

/1

What do you call a clever horse stumbling?
donkey!

/1

what do you call a talkative hen?
a parrot hen

/1

JOKES TOTAL   /4

JOKESTER 1

What did the hot dog say to the hamburger?
Let's sandwich it!

/1

What did the chef dinosaur cook for the competition?
a volcano cake!

/1

What time does a duck go to school?
At the quack time

/1

Why did the eggs break?
They saw a comedy movie!

/1

 **JOKES TOTAL** /4

pass the book to jokester 2! ➡

JOKESTER 2

where do flowers go every time?
to the wedding!

/1

what do you call a smart dog?
poodle

/1

why did the polar bear lose his teeth?
he ate a frozen fish

/1

what kind of food do cows like to eat?
grass sandwich!

/1

 JOKES TOTAL   /4

JOKESTER 2

What did the old lady say to the policeman? /1
I lose my boring cat, find it!

What did the envelope say to his friends? /1
we will go to places!

what did happen when the dragon fart? /1
everything run!

what did ants do every night? /1
telling jokes!

JOKES TOTAL /4

time to add up your points! ➡

SCORE BOARD

In each jokester's add total jokes
points for this round!

JOKESTER 1

/8

_____

TOTAL

JOKESTER 2

/8

_____

TOTAL

_____

ROUND 1 WINNER

FINAL SCORE BOARD

	jokester 1 /8	jokester 2 /8
Round 1		
Round 2		
Round 3		
Round 4		
Round 5		
Round 6		
Round 7		
Round 8		
Round 9		
Round 10		
Round 11		
Total		

THE CHAMPION IS:

_____

Congradulation!

CHEK OUT OUR

Visit our Amazon store at:

OTHER JOKE BOOKS!

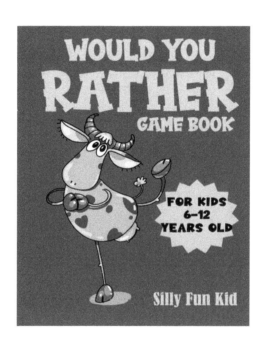

www.Amazon.com/author/sillyfunkid